GROUNDWATER III A COLLECTION OF POETRY, QUOTES AND MEDITATIONS

ERICA L. HAMMOND

ISBN:9798430213497

DEDICATION

To: Mr. Patterson, My ninth-grade teacher. I loved being in your classroom. We walked in the spirit; The experience gave me clear vision to succeed in life.

To: The Audience, Understand that these concepts are in your core. They were there first. We all share spirit; we are God. Again: This is our nature, our heavens and universe(s) to heart.
A note to the Audience: I like to use Ebonics as a primary language; It is mixed with standard English. Have patience, it is a broken language. I like to use common (slave) speech. For example: I like to capitalize powers. I like to uncapitalize powers. It takes patience to read. It is a beautiful work. Also, when you come to the Meditation Chapter, remember to: Cross your arm over your chest / core and allow yourself to feel your connection to the heavens and the universe(s). Thanks, Erica LaShaun Hammond

CONTENTS

ACKNOWLEDGMENTS

To: My Mother and Father, Kathleen and Erik Thornton. I would like to thank you for the financial support and the care you've given me over the years. You are respected and loved.
"Cloverleaf."

1 CHAPTER FRIENDSHIP

Friendship

1.

Your love helps me with living.
It helps sustain my soul; I can present myself to others and they find liveliness in my bones.

Uniquely beautiful

2.

My good friend- I think of you always-I send words to comfort you.
You are something. A talent in this world.
You are beautiful in spirit, generous and a kind soul.
You are truly something- a bloom- flower.
Dear woman, you bring beauty uniquely to this world.

3.

In this life, on this journey around the sun,
My thoughts returned to you my friend, always:
I find time and again, my soul is wholly restored.

Poor friends

4.

If you need wealth, have poor friends. Their insights and wisdoms run deep. If your poor friends do not have wisdom, pray.
No!
Talk them into wearing their natural crowns.

Separation.

5.

It was a good friendship, tested and true.
I move on from you, from this leg of life's journey.
Distance from you is like a form of death.

6.

My friend, my soul is happy to return to you. I make my plans to life and living accordingly.

7.

I am open. I am learnt.
Link to me, be a friend.

8.

I get to walk through desolation, the nether world with you:
I promise to be centered, in peace with you, on a better plane.

The Whole Picture

9.

I am that puzzle piece missing in your heart, my love. Just know that I will carry it and always willing to place it back, my friend.

2 CHAPTER OLDER IN AGE

10.

I am feeling blessed as I work: Always with you (leg) in mind.

11.

I rise.
I stand, from youth to old.
I am a person, seeking to counsel others as an older woman.
Accept me.
Forgive me for time lost; understand
I come.
(Open your hearts and minds.)

12.

I know every slave man looks at his
children with:
Pride.
Faith.
Disappointment.
Hope.
Direction and newfound clarity
for themselves.

13.

I care for the world:
I post.
I find my station in life.

14.

The hardest part of failure is the forgotten inner child.
How does one explain life and happenstance
to the spirited part of oneself?

15.

Time has changed, in youth, I assumed it would.
Am I ready for trial by fire:
No!
I am resourceful and will respond with work ahead.

16.

I was self-centered in life, overgrown.
On that course, I found myself broken, overtime in this world.
I have faith in (G)gods.
(They are the kings of Thrones.)
With grace, I am posted, healing and beautiful.

17.

Jealousy is nature's face, and it is telling. Let it help you find (truths) you can advance with.

18.

I Am:
I find a way to be.
I am old.
I start my quest to recapture youth:
To be viable, true and hardy at this age.

19.

I battle in mind;
Through so much, I find myself- old- something.
I sit at the fountain of youth,
daydreaming.
Staring back at a reflection of a dreaded life.
A tear, single, escapes my eye.
I stir the water, my wish, to head time.

20.

Redemption,
nature,
original,
are in my soul:
See me!
We have a duty to bare our souls to the world.

21.

I am writing: I am a teacher (common.)
Don't judge, because I am late.

3 CHAPTER LOVE

22.

Love: It's good.
I wonder?
I'm invested; What will it bare me?
I've cultivated love.
I've respected its seasons.
I planted and tended to its needs.
I'm due:
Yes, I want a great harvest.
I've worked for this: love.

23.

To love is the way of life. It's amazing to spread fire from soul to soul.
(Truly heaven community.)

24.

I want love; I shall love myself.
I bestowed these common things in my life.
My mind runs:
A walk in the rain.
Picking wine berries from the bushes.
Biking.
Picking flowers.
Peacefully drinking mullein tea...

25.

My love for you is amazing:
Platonic.
Life-giving.

(I loved you instantly.)

We could be:
Stronger
Better.
Accountable.
Working.
Something.
Together.
(Coalesced.)

Now that's love.

26.

Unconditional love:
I will explore my internal dimensions.
Learnt,
(I will evolve.)

4 CHAPTER HOMELESS

27.

I am homeless, a wanderer in spirit.
(I am a man.)
I bless the earth!
I take up ruling and circumstance.

28.

(I am a ruler. I am great.)
I go from slave to wanderer.

29.

We are a Human Organism; Work sustains the soul.

The Tithe

30.

Do you give? It is important to do.
I'm a giver to community.
I joined with people who make it
a better place, land.
(I've become a transformer of the world.)

31.

Homeless, yet still a ruler.
I feel the energy from my core.

(I am.)

32.

Millions upon millions are invested in:
Welfare, housing, Medicare...
What we need, Oh Mighty Government/ gods,
is investment in better laws helping jobs to stay in the USA
for Colored-Americans.
Asia shines back
(we are learning.)

33.

Do you believe in yourself?
Look the homeless in the face, note the reflection:
Is it still trusting?

NATURE AND MAKEUP

34.

(G)gods are aligned with me: The homeless.

35.

What do (G)gods want with me?
Homeless, lost in voids, yet still aligned and walking with God.

36.

If societies needs its bottoms, it is disqualifying world.

37.

Homeless;
The bottom, where I find I'm a Lost King.
(I am still the ruler over circumstances.)
I am a wanderer in the spirit;
Lost.
Someday-
self expectantly-
all shall watch me fit my crown.

38.

I was a slave of Labor- breaking that yoke-
I now am set free.
Today, I am nearly homeless.
I'm finding my body, the new enemy.
My God, have mercy;
Infinity hear me!
I'm struck, cursed, in pain:
Please be lenient!

39.

I am free from a job of (slave labor.)
I will use this time to plant seeds and grow a great harvest;
(I am a preacher.)
Think to bless a woman of (G)god.
System
should invest in its people.

40.

I'm nearly homeless;
I wrestle hard with my body.

It wants... so many things.
(I am the head of this being.)

I fight, as a human being, A god.
I can't be a subject slave.

5 CHAPTER MOTHERHOOD

41.

I am a parent; I have done it.
Be pleased with me.
It is all that I have envisioned
(death and it's coming.)
My dreams have come to pass,
although black and dark.
We, however, live in truth.

42.

My Son, My spirit spars with you;
I ask for your forgiveness.
Together we have barren fields.
I search deep and find, with failure we are natural
testaments of our times.

43.

I had a son; He is a light.
He inspires me, from creation on.
His light gives me wisdom to connect to worlds.
Amen.
I am a Mother- a graced- teacher.
I am knowledgeable with experienced life.

6 CHAPTER SELF

44.

Life revolves around (yourself.)
I am: Orbiting around my decisions, my choices, my facts of life.
I am: A cold, distant, glowing planet.
I want you to know my hues (characteristics) and admire them.

45.

I don't have a face;
I don't have a (desired) identity.
So I self-educate: piece.
I give: piece.
I eat bread and drink water (spiritually and simply) piece.
I merged with the (learning) community: piece.
Piecing myself together:
Becoming.

46.

I believe in myself.
I love where I've been.
I am aligned with time, imperfect:
But there.
Time runs both ways, I've been found true.
I am a believer in myself as a hero;
It's wonderful.

47.

Where I can't be self-sufficient there is no peace.
Where respect, love and pride dwell: I have to arrive and be among the (blessed) and the counted.

48.

I stir my spirit, draw from its well and satisfy my needs.
So Good.
Wonderfully satisfying:
I am.

7 CHAPTER ABUSE

49.

I need them to remember me, as I have surfaced in this life.
The water from the well of life,
although bitter,
is alright from time to time.

50.

Abuse.
Amazing: A person is a well.
Storing every memory and mineralized treasured thought.
Living water, livelihood.
Life:
A living well.
How bitter it is not to be able to use the water from the well of the soul. By being aches.
I am of thirst.

8 CHAPTER YOUTH

51.

Dear youth, relatability is a fine golden crown.

52.

I remember You.
Talking and reaching out to the community.
Crossing tracks, talking to others.
Your spirit is great, you are hope (a piece) in the lands.
(I want you to remember that.)

Such wonderful memories,
a sweet water well; I can drink and be glad.

Garden Of Life

53.

I walk into the garden of life.
I see a gold, jeweled, chalice.
It is filled to the brim with:
Living water.
I am curious, so I drink, deeply.
It is enough:
I'd let it quench my thirst.
I let it cool my core.
I let it absorb from head to toes.
I drink to life:
I am whole. I have changed.
I am restored.
Yes, I am (G)god.
(I am that living water.)

54.

We are old.
We are yesterday's generation. Our time is passing, yet we are still engaged. You are our youth.
You are the days present force. Remember this council: make sure you are understandable.

55.

Eye to eye, truth to truth. Old and young, torches shall be created and passed. (Be open to both.)

56.

Wisdom:
Dear youth, be relatable.
Captivate all ages.
Inherently, we shall respect all ages

.

57.

Slavery,
low wages, gun violence,
failing schools,
hypocritical churches, and so on:
I am an aging youth.
I declare,
I am young, but somehow still very old.

58.

I am content.
I look back on my youth and smile.
In my older (young) years,
I considered you wise.
The well of memories I have, the water is fine.
I give water from this well, to others, amazing.
I'm a Minister.
The water is good- my life- nourishes on.

9 CHAPTER DEATH

59.

There is a spirit fusion between us:
You are a part of me. Even in death, My Father,
you are in mind, heart, and spirit:
Always with me.

60.

Oh Father, with death, there is a cord to you.
I let you rest a good while before:
In struggle and war,
I help your spirit rise to its former glory.
We will walk in a land of knowledge/ Heaven,
together as one, in harmony.

61.

Our Father, you are loved.
I remember your familiarity:
A wonderful living orb.
You plugged into our lives; We are blessed.
If you depart, my soul will rest.
Your sacrifice and your life are stored treasures in heart.
I will find it a pleasure to see your flesh and spirit strong (again)
Our Father rest with earth until then.

10 CHAPTER TRUE GOD

62.

Silver,
White, Brown, Black,
Gold:
Beautiful, the clay-colored Face of
Our God.

Declaration

63.

As a man, I shall link. I will serve you.
Spirit,
You shall be my God.

(Reminder: cross your arms over your (chest /core) and connect to the heavens and the universe(s.)

64.

I Am.
My soul is a kaleidoscope of wonders.
Nature:
I marvel you!
The universe: To know you more.

65.

Life.
Memories and time with family, friends and foes:
(The promised land.)

66.

Nature and (G)gods in harmony.
I sing of unity.
I worship, I sing. I praise.

67.

I am God.
I decree: To be a balancer of light and dark.

68.

I care for you as god: It reflects in my service.

69.

I am humbled.
I am proud.
You are worthy of my call,
duty and service.
Oh, spirit,
You have desires, needs and are available
I shall make you, my God.

70.

Minister,
I watch you lay your hands on me.
You are hued in spirit with (G)gods.
Hallelujah!

Kingdom

71.

I see the people on a vast plain,
where we are created the same, in strength and glories.
What comes next is separating men, women and gods.
(Kingdoms shall rise.)

72.

I am aligned with (G)gods.
Moreover, My entire being cries:
Glory, Hallelujah!

73.

I am nearly to the top of the mountain.
I've come to find success.
I dare to meet lively people and habiting rich culture there.
I've come to this mountain,
a leader to dwell.
I've come for becoming and leadership.
I know, the gods made this system.
Arriving,
I find lost kingly people.
Discovering lost heads and broken bones.

74.

Spirit show me your face.
I am a servant; I will plan for you.

11 CHAPTER MEDITATION

75.

Oh, soul.
I am glad you believe;
You have peace with my crown and throne.
I am god as one and God as a whole.

76.

Oh, Glory of glories.
Hallelujah.
Amen.
I am one. I am many: The face of the Lord.

77.

My body: A tree.
I have a healthy mind, spirit, and soul.
I am a tree.
I will be. I will bare beauty. I will bare fruit.

78.

I am relieved;
(I can Be.)
I am God; I can stand alone.

Sun

79.

The Sun,
she bestows gifts upon me. She touches me with her grace.
I feel prized and renewed by her daily. I will challenge her
throughout my days.

80.

Love:
Center me. Restore me.
Renew me.
I am yours to have.
You are mine to take:
Love.

Anew

81.

I am delighted and formed...
I'm realizing my worth.
I've always had a small imagination of my being.
But oh, the surprises of the universe, I have found
centeredly that I am god.

Extra

82.

The Forest is intriguing.
I see God's design. I will give Her (the forest)
my heart, soul and mind.
I will learn Her ways, the Forest, so that I
understand nature.
She is amazing, her connections-
worldwide- are awe inspiring.
I want to serve nature; I want to grow.
I want to know my place
in the world.

Extra

83.

Redemption, grace and faith are embodied in the life force of the mighty tree.

ABOUT THE AUTHOR

I live in Akron, OH. I have lived here all my life. I am the mother of two adult, young men. I am a divorced woman. I am 44 years of age. I am a lover of the arts and poetry. I am proud to be releasing the GROUNDWATER series. It is a dream come true.

Made in the USA
Middletown, DE
18 March 2022